Name: _____

Class: _____

Teacher: _____

Islamic Studies
Textbook Level 3

Minhaj-ul-Quran International

Published by

Minhaj-ul-Quran Publications
30 Brindley Road
Manchester
M16 9HQ (UK)

Acknowledgements

Bilal Hussain, Safina Nazir, Muhammad Zeeshan Qadri, Ali Akbar, Raffiq Patel and M. Dawood Mehmood

A sincere thank you to Ajmal Khan for his assistance in the design work

ISBN: 978-1-908229-57-1

www.minhajpublications.com

www.islamforkids.org.uk

First published August 2018

Printed by Elma Printing in Turkey

proudly sponsored by
letsREVIVE
a project of Minhaj Welfare Foundation
minhajwelfare.org
Registered in England & Wales 1084057. Scotland SC043566

Islamic Studies
Textbook Level 3

Series Editors

Waqas Ahmed Amin

Jawed Iqbal Tahiri

Mariam Khalid

Series Director

Tahseen Khalid

Minhaj-ul-Quran International

Preface

In the name of Allah, the Most Merciful, the Most Kind.

WE PRAISE ALLAH that the Muslim community has come a long way since the days when the first immigrants settled in Britain. From that time till today, there have been significant developments in the quality of educational material being produced by British Muslims. Many advancements have been made in this regard such that English is fast becoming one of the academic languages of Islam, alongside Arabic, Persian, Urdu and Turkish.

The importance of education cannot be overstated. The British Muslim community has put great effort into imparting Islamic knowledge to their children. Islamic classes and religious seminaries have been established up and down the country for the single goal of teaching the coming generations the fundamentals of their religion. Among those that have been at the forefront in this regard is Minhaj-ul-Quran International, a global organisation with branches in over 90 countries.

As an organisation, Minhaj-ul-Quran International seeks to uplift Muslims worldwide through the revival of education and spirituality. It established its first branch in the United Kingdom in the late 1980s and founded its first centre in the 1990s. For more than two decades it has endeavoured to provide for the educational and spiritual needs of the Muslim diaspora of Great Britain.

The 'Islam for Kids' initiative is part of the longstanding services of Minhaj-ul-Quran International. This Islamic Studies series was produced and developed by second and third generation British scholars, who are trained classically in the traditional Islamic sciences, alongside QTS (Qualified Teaching Status) accredited teachers. It is an indigenous and local endeavour by the UK branch of Minhaj-ul-Quran International to fulfil the educational needs of native English-speaking students.

The Syllabus

The 'Islam for Kids' Islamic Studies series has been split into six levels with each level corresponding to the years of the state-funded education system in the UK. It is recommended to start level one at the age of 5 when the child starts year one at primary school and to complete level 6 by the age of 11 when the child completes his or her primary school education. However, the series can be started earlier at an earlier age or later depending on the ability of the student.

The six levels have been grouped into three stages, with each stage consisting of two levels. In the first stage, which consists of levels one and two, the aim is to ease the child into understanding Islamic concepts and terminology. The purpose of this stage is not to burden the child with technical knowledge about Islam, but rather to simply instil in them a sense of Muslim identity and to explore key Islamic concepts.

Traditionally, Muslim parents have been advised to have a play-based approach with their children's learning for the first seven years and then to formally teach them for the next seven years. Following this advice, in the first two years of the syllabus, a more visual approach has been adopted with the text being kept at a minimum. This enables the content to be taught in a child-friendly manner and allows teachers and parents to make the lessons more interactive and engaging for the child.

The second stage of the syllabus begins at level three when the child reaches seven years of age. From this level onwards, a more formal approach to learning is adopted. Many of the concepts in the first stage are revisited, but instead of being largely pictorial, they are more text-based so that the key concepts can be conveyed in detail to the child and to encourage the child to start thinking about the content in more depth.

In the third stage of the syllabus, which consists of levels five and six, the series shifts to a more text-heavy approach. This is to encourage the child to learn independently and practice their key reading and comprehension skills. The content at this level increases in difficulty to engage students academically and to raise the standard of literacy and understanding of Islamic concepts.

The concepts from the previous two stages are revisited in this third stage but in much more detail. Parents and teachers alike will find this stage beneficial as reading material to help prepare in terms of subject knowledge for teaching the lessons in the earlier two stages. In this way, the three stages work together to ease the child into becoming well acquainted with Islamic terminology, concepts and values.

By the end of this syllabus, the child will have acquired the essential Islamic knowledge (*Fard `Ayn*) for them to be able to live their life as a practising Muslim. This Islamic Studies series is an excellent resource for parents to lay the foundation for their child's learning. If Allah wills, further levels will be added to this syllabus, thus enhancing the child's understanding of Islam and enabling them to become lifelong learners of the Islamic tradition.

The First Edition

In preparation of this series, authentic and reliable content was taken from the works of great scholars who represent Islamic orthodoxy. Some of the books that were consulted in the creation of the content were:

- Imam ash-Shurunbulali's *Nur al-Idah* and its commentary, *Maraqi al-Falah*

- Imam al-Laqqani's *Jawharah at-Tawhid*

- Shaykh Salih Farfur's *ar-Risalah an-Nafi`ah fi `Ilm at-Tawhid*

- Imam Ibn Hisham's *as-Sirah an-Nabawiyyah* (including its English rendition by Martin Lings)

- Imam Ibn Kathir's *al-Bidayah wa an-Nihayah*

- and the many hadith collections compiled by the founder of Minhaj-ul-Quran, Shaykh-ul-Islam Dr Muhammad Tahir-ul-Qadri

The contents of these books have been adapted for children at an age appropriate level while keeping in consideration the specific needs and requirements of Western Muslims.

We are eager to hear from the wider community and to gain feedback regarding the series. For this purpose, we have set up an email address where you can tell us your views and suggestions. You can contact us at the following address: **feedback@fmriuk.org**.

Acknowledgements

Before closing, I would like to thank my co-editors, Jawed Iqbal Tahiri and Mariam Khalid, for their commitment and assistance in helping to prepare and develop the contents of this syllabus. I would also like to thank the Series Director, Tahseen Khalid, for his great determination and support in bringing this series to fruition.

I would also like to thank Bilal Hussain, for his assistance in preparing the outline of the syllabus, and the Textbook Review Team (Safina Nazir, Muhammad Zeeshan Qadri, Ali Akbar, Raffiq Patel and Dawood Mehmood) for their feedback and support. A special thank you goes to Ajmal Khan for the outstanding devotion he has shown in improving and further developing the design work.

I pray to Allah that He accepts our efforts and makes it a means of salvation for us in this life and the next, and we pray that this series becomes a means of uplifting the Ummah for generations to come.

Amin bi-jahi Sayyid al-Mursalin ﷺ

Waqas Ahmed Amin
Minhaj-ul-Quran Publications
1st Dhu al-Hijjah 1439 AH/12th August 2018 CE

Contents

Allah, the All Powerful

Allah is the **All-Powerful**. This means that there is nothing and nobody else who has the same power as Him.

Allah has all the power. He is the **Most-Powerful** and no one has power equal to or more than Him.

Everything happens by the will and power of Allah. He is '**al-Malik**' – the King, who controls everything.

Every time the rain falls, the wind blows, the sun shines or a flower grows, Allah's Power is controlling it.

Every time you move, eat, drink, walk, talk and play, Allah's Power is allowing you to do that. We do not do anything all by ourselves, whatever we do it is because Allah gives us the power to do it.

The power we have is only from Allah, because it is Allah Who makes that power for us. We cannot do anything unless Allah makes it happen.

Allah is so powerful that only by saying the word '**Be!**' He made everything in this world and the whole universe when there was nothing.

The Qur'an tells us:

o   The heavens and the earth belong to Allah alone, and Allah has perfect control and power over everything.

o   Allah is the Most Powerful and the Almighty.

o   Allah creates whatever He wants.

o   We need Allah, but Allah does not need us. Allah does not need anyone or anything.

o   If Allah wanted to, He could make human beings go away and make a new creation. This is not hard for Allah to do.

Prophet Muhammad ﷺ told us all about Allah. He said:

o   Allah is always fair, so we should always be fair to each other.

o   Only Allah can help us, so we should pray to Allah to help us to be good Muslims.

o   Only Allah can feed us, so we should pray to Allah to give us food.

o   Only Allah can give us clothes, so we should pray to Allah to give us clothes.

o   Only Allah can forgive us when we do bad things, so we should pray to Allah for forgiveness.

o   We cannot help or harm Allah. Even if Allah gave us everything we asked for, it would not lessen Allah's power.

o   Our deeds are recorded, and Allah will judge us for them. Those who do good deeds should praise and thank Allah and those who do not should only blame themselves.

Who are the Prophets?

Ever since Allah made human beings, He sent special people to deliver His message, so that people know how to live in a way that makes Him happy. These special people who delivered Allah's message were the '**Prophets**' and '**Messengers**'.

Those who accept the teachings given to us by the Prophets and Messengers are known as the **believers** because they believe in the message of Allah. Whereas those who reject their message are known as the **disbelievers** because they deny Allah's message.

We cannot receive Allah's message on our own, so Allah sent Prophets to give His message to us. The Prophets were sent to teach us and help us to be good in this life.

Allah's Prophets are special people. They are the best. They are the most beautiful people Allah made, in the way they look and behave.

They are chosen and loved by Allah.

Allah spoke to them when He sent down His message to them, telling them how to help and teach people.

There are several important things we need to know about them.

1. The Prophets are always truthful; they never lie.

2. The Prophets always obey Allah; they never do anything wrong.

3. The Prophets are very smart and intelligent.

4. The Prophets teach people about Allah. They tell people what Allah wants them to do and how He wants them to worship and obey Him.

5. The Prophets teach people to be good and to be kind to everyone. They tell people to care for all creatures and to be respectful to all things.

The first of the Prophets was Prophet **Adam** ﷺ. He was also the first human being made by Allah.

The last of the Prophets was our **Prophet Muhammad** ﷺ.

Prophet Muhammad ﷺ was also the greatest and best of all the Prophets. No prophet will be born after him.

In between Prophet Adam ﷺ and Prophet Muhammad ﷺ, Allah Almighty sent thousands of Prophets. So many Prophets were sent to all parts of the world that we do not know the exact number.

We believe in them all. We love and respect all of the Prophets.

Amongst the Prophets that were sent, there were five who were the most special. They are known as the '**Mighty Five**' and they were:

1. Prophet Nuh ﷺ

2. Prophet Ibrahim ﷺ

3. Prophet Musa ﷺ

4. Prophet `Isa ﷺ

5. Prophet Muhammad ﷺ

Peace and blessings be upon them all.

What to Say and When? (Part 1)

Greeting a Muslim

When we meet another Muslim, we say, '**As-Salaamu `Alaykum**'; which means 'Peace be upon you.'

When we reply, we say, '**Wa `Alaykumus-Salaam**', which means, 'And peace be upon you too'.

The Sunnah Manners of Meeting

o Always try to be the first person to say, 'As-Salaamu `Alaykum'.

o Face the person that you are saying Salam to.

o Give Salam to people who you know and also to people who you do not know in the same way.

o Do not reply by signaling with the head, hand or fingers.

o A standing person should give Salam to a sitting person.

o The person who is walking should give salam to the person who is standing still.

o The younger person should give Salam to the elder person.

o Say, 'As-Salaamu `Alaykum', out aloud before entering a room or house.

o When giving Salam to a group of people make sure you include everyone.

When Starting Something

Before we begin an important task, we must say, **'Bismillaahir Rahmaanir Raheem'**, which means: 'In the Name of Allah, the Most Merciful, the Most Kind.' When we say this, Allah rewards us and puts blessings in our actions so that our task becomes easier for us.

Prophet Muhammad ﷺ told us to say 'Bismillaah' so that our actions can be perfect and complete.

When we say, '**Bismillah**' (In the Name of Allah), the Shaytan gets angry and he does not want to be near us. When we forget to say it, he becomes happy and wants to stay close to us. So, we must always remember to say '**Bismillaahir Rahmaanir Raheem**' and ask Allah to protect us from Shaytan.

When Should We Say Bismillah?

Before performing Wudu'.

Before having a bath.

Before brushing our teeth.

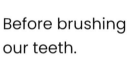

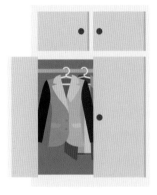

Before putting on our clothes.

Before starting the Prayer (Salah).

Before reading the Holy Qur'an.

Before travelling or going on a journey.

Before eating and drinking

Before going to sleep

Before starting our school work.

Allah, the Creator

In the beginning, before anything was made, Allah existed alone. Then, Allah decided that He would make everything else, and so, with His great Power, He began to make things. Allah made things by saying the word '**Be**', and they would be made, out of nothing.

In this way, Allah created the rivers and seas, the shining sun, the glowing moon, the strong mountains, and the big blue sky. He created birds, trees, flowers and human beings. He made a man out of clay and then breathed life into the clay model and in this way, Prophet Adam ﷺ was made.

Prophet Adam ﷺ was the first human being that Allah made. For this reason, Adam ﷺ is known as the father of all human beings. Then, Allah made Lady Hawwa', the mother of all human beings.

Allah made human beings to be the best creation and raised them above everything else that He made. He gave us eyes to see the beautiful forms He created and ears to hear all the pleasant sounds. He gave us a brain and a heart so that we may come to know His signs and blessings.

Human beings are the most special creation of Allah, and so He made everything on the earth for us:

- Allah made the sun to keep us warm and to make plants and trees grow.

- Allah made water for us to drink when we are thirsty and to water the soil so that trees and plants grow.

- Allah made trees for delicious fruits to grow on, so we can eat the fruit. Trees also protect us from the hot sun.

- Allah made plants. Flowers grow from plants and they are pretty to look at.

- Allah made the mountains to protect us from storms and large waves of water from the oceans. This keeps us and our homes safe. Mountains also help to make sure the earth does not shake.

We are Allah's special creation, so we should look after everything that Allah has made for us. We must believe in Allah and thank Him for everything, because He is the One Who created everything. One of Allah Almighty's Beautiful Names is '**al-Khaliq**' (the Maker and Creator).

Allah the Creator

Prophet Adam ﷺ

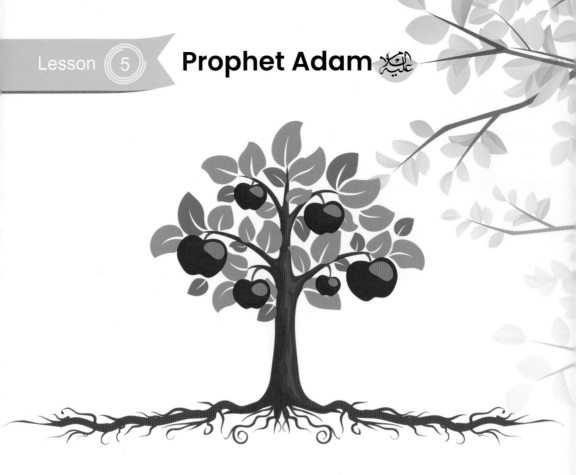

After Allah created Prophet Adam ﷺ, He created the first woman, Lady Hawwa'. Allah made Prophet Adam ﷺ the father of all human beings and He made Lady Hawwa' their mother. In this way, every person who was born after them are their children. No matter how someone looks like or where they are from, we are all from the same human family and are the children of Adam ﷺ.

Prophet Adam ﷺ and Lady Hawwa' lived happily together in Paradise (Jannah), where they enjoyed its gardens, its flowing rivers of milk and honey, its fruits and foods, and more than anything else, they enjoyed Allah's closeness and friendship.

Allah planned that human beings will live on earth. So, one day Allah wanted to test Prophet Adam ﷺ and Lady Hawwa'. He ordered them saying, "O Adam! You and your wife may live in Paradise (Jannah), and eat from wherever you both want. But do not go near this one tree, because if you do then you will be among the people who do wrong."

So, they lived and ate from Paradise (Jannah), but they never went near that one tree, because Allah had told them not to as a test.

However, the Shaytan, who had been thrown out of Paradise (Jannah) because he did not respect Prophet Adam ﷺ, was still angry, arrogant and very jealous. He wanted Prophet Adam ﷺ and Lady Hawwa' to fail in this test Allah had set them.

So, one day, the Shaytan came and tricked Prophet Adam ﷺ and Lady Hawwa' into eating from the forbidden tree.

He lied to them, saying, "The only reason Allah has told you not to eat from this tree is because if you do, you will become angels and you will stay here in Allah's closeness forever and ever."

"I promise you that I'm telling the truth. I am your friend and only want what is best for you!" he continued, making a false promise.

Prophet Adam ﷺ and Lady Hawwa' who loved Allah and His company, wanted to stay in His closeness forever. So, they were tricked by the Shaytan's false promise and ate from the tree.

As soon as they ate from the tree, they realised that they had made a mistake, and they began to feel very sad and sorry.

After that, Allah Almighty sent Prophet Adam ﷺ and Lady Hawwa' to the earth, to worship Him and to care and look after the earth.

Prophet Adam ﷺ and Lady Hawwa' who were very sad and sorry about their mistake, begged Allah to forgive them and be pleased with them.

Because He is the Most Kind and the Most Merciful, Allah Almighty gifted them with special words, which they could read and get forgiveness from Him.

The words were:

رَبَّنَا ظَلَمْنَا أَنفُسَنَا وَإِن لَّمْ تَغْفِرْ لَنَا وَتَرْحَمْنَا لَنَكُونَنَّ مِنَ الْخَاسِرِينَ

'Our Lord. We have done wrong to ourselves; and if you do not forgive us, and be kind to us, we will be among the losers.'

Prophet Adam عليه السلام and Lady Hawwa' repeated these words, and Allah forgave them. Allah told them that they will stay on the earth for a short while, and then return to Paradise (Jannah) forever after death.

They lived on the earth for many years and had many children. Their children married and spread over the entire earth, and in this way, the human family grew bigger and spread out in far and distant places across the earth.

Cleanliness (Keeping Clean)

As a Muslim, it is very important to always stay clean. This is because Prophet Muhammad ﷺ told us that Allah Himself is the Most-Pure and Clean, and He loves those who are pure and clean.

Prophet Muhammad ﷺ was the purest human being ever born. Even when he was a child, he was always clean, smelled nice and kept his room clean and tidy.

Prophet Muhammad ﷺ told us to wash ourselves every day, have a bath regularly and brush our teeth often during the day.

The Arabic word for cleanliness is '**Taharah**'. To have Taharah we must do the following things.

1. Keeping MYSELF clean:

Wash away any dirt on the body.

Perform Istin-ja' well.

Brush the teeth in the morning and night.

Wash hands and face when waking up in the morning.

Rinse the mouth after eating.

Wash face, hands, arms, feet if they are dirty.

Have a shower or a bath regularly.

Try to stay in Wudu' all the time.

Wear perfume to smell nice.

Wear clothes that are neat, clean and smell nice.

Change underwear and socks regularly.

2. Keeping my ENVIRONMENT clean:

Clean your bedroom and keep it tidy.

Keep all your things neat and organised.

Do not throw rubbish in the house.

Do not throw rubbish in the Mosque.

Do not make a mess when eating food.

Always clean up after yourself when you can.

Do not throw rubbish in school.

Always use bins and bags for any rubbish.

3. Keeping the WORLD clean:

a. Do not throw rubbish on the streets or anywhere outside.
b. Always use bins for rubbish.
c. Pick up any rubbish when you can.
d. Do not pick flowers or leaves from plants or trees.
e. Recycle things like cardboard, tin cans and paper.

The Hadith Jibra'il

One day, the Sahabah (the Prophet's Companions – Allah be pleased with them) were sitting with Prophet Muhammad ﷺ, when, suddenly, a stranger appeared. It was almost as though he appeared out of nowhere. But there he was, a man, walking towards them from the desert around the blessed city of Madinah.

He was wearing clean white clothes and had black hair. Although the man was a complete stranger to the Companions, it did not appear as though he had travelled from outside Madinah, because his clothes did not have dust on them, and he did not look tired.

The man continued walking, until he reached the place where the Companions were sitting. He calmly walked passed all the Companions and went directly to Prophet Muhammad ﷺ. With the greatest respect and love, he kneeled and sat in front of Prophet Muhammad ﷺ, placing his knees against the Prophet's blessed knees and his hands on the Prophet's blessed thighs.

The man then leaned forward towards the Prophet ﷺ and said, "O Muhammad, what is Islam?"

The Prophet ﷺ replied, "Islam is that you believe there is no God but Allah, and that Muhammad is Allah's Messenger; and that you perform the prayer; give Charity; fast in Ramadan, and perform the Pilgrimage if you are able to."

"You have spoken the truth," responded the strange man.

The Companions were surprised that he said that. The stranger asked the question and then he himself said that the answer was correct. The Companions found this very strange. Who was this stranger? And how was he able to know that the Prophet's answer was correct?

The stranger then continued asking questions about other teachings of Islam. Every time Prophet Muhammad ﷺ, replied, the stranger would agree with the answer, saying, "You have spoken the truth,"

The Companions listened with interest. They were amazed at this stranger and everything about him.

Eventually, the stranger finished questioning the Prophet ﷺ. He got up and left the gathering.

The Companions – Allah be pleased with them – learnt so much from the good questions asked by this stranger and they really wanted to know who he was. However, out of respect for the Prophet ﷺ, they did not ask. They knew that if it was important for them to know, then the Prophet ﷺ would tell them himself.

In fact, part of the Prophet's kindness and care for his Companions was that he would never hide any helpful knowledge from them; he would tell them everything that they needed to know.

So, the Companions stayed quiet. Some of the Companions quickly went out following the stranger, but he was nowhere to be found. They searched and searched, but it was like he had disappeared into thin air. The Companions were even more surprised. He had disappeared as suddenly as he had appeared! Who was this man?

The Prophet ﷺ knew that the Companions were interested in knowing who the stranger was. And so after a few days, he asked his great Companion 'Umar, "O 'Umar! Do you know who the questioner was that day?" `Umar replied, "Allah and His Messenger know best."

The Prophet ﷺ then told them who the stranger was. He said, "That was the Angel Jibra'il. He came down to teach you your religion."

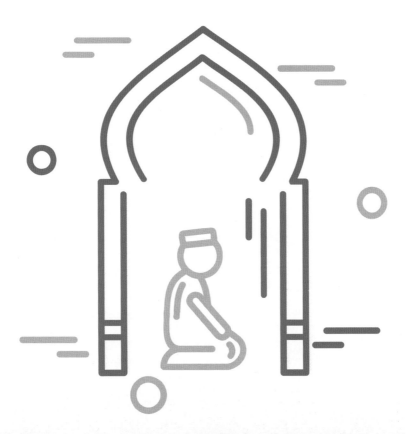

The Five Pillars

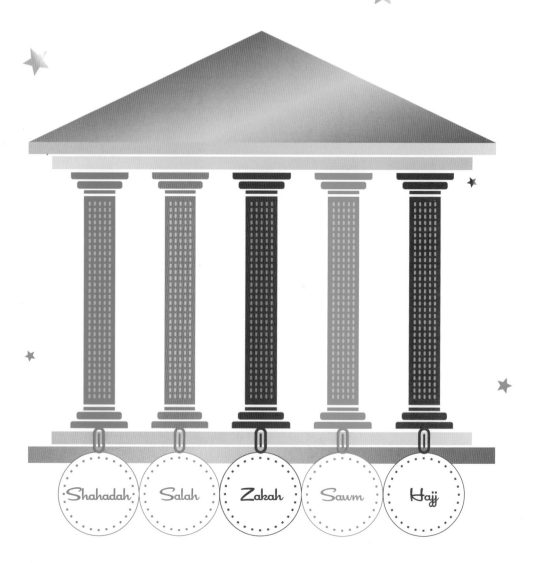

Shahadah | Salah | Zakah | Sawm | Hajj

Islam is built on five things. These are known as the '**Five Pillars of Islam**'.

Imagine Islam as a tent; a tent has four poles at its four corners, and it has one pole in the middle. These poles are very important to set up the tent. They hold the tent up. Without the poles, the tent would fall to the ground.

Or, imagine a building. If the walls and pillars that hold the building up are taken away, then the building will fall over and just be a pile of bricks.

The Five Pillars of Islam are like the poles of the tent, or the walls and pillars of a building. They make Islam strong and hold it up in the life of a Muslim.

If a Muslim does not follow the five pillars of Islam, then in that Muslim's life Islam will start to break down.

The Five Pillars of Islam are five things that every Muslim must do to be a true and good Muslim.

The Five Pillars of Islam are:

1. **Shahadah:** To say and believe that there is no God but Allah, and that Muhammad is Allah's Messenger.

2. **Salah:** Praying five times a day, at times that have been given to us by Allah.

3. **Zakah:** Giving money to poor people as charity.

4. **Sawm:** Fasting in the holy month of Ramadan (the 9th Islamic month).

5. **Hajj:** Travelling to Makkah to the Ka'bah, to perform the Pilgrimage.

The Muslim who does these five things keeps Islam strong and standing in their life. He or she protects their Islam and stops it from breaking down.

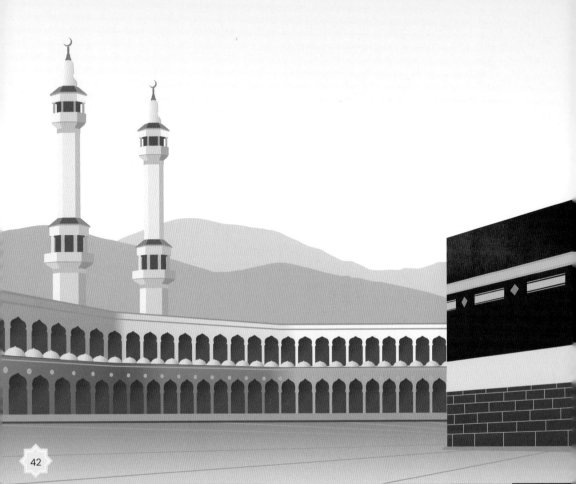

The **Shahadah** stays with you all the time, in every moment of your life. Your belief is in your heart; a safe secret that never leaves you.

The **Salah** is done every day; five times a day.

The **Zakah** is done once a year, if you have extra money to give away.

The **Sawm** is done once a year, for a whole month, in Ramadan.

The **Hajj** is done at least once in your whole life, if you have money and good health.

The First Pillar of Islam: The Shahadah

The **Shahadah** is when a Muslim says and believes that there is no God other than Allah, and that Muhammad ﷺ is Allah's Messenger.

The Shahadah

أَشْهَدُ أَنْ لَّا إِلَهَ إِلَّا اللّٰهُ وَحْدَهُ لَا شَرِيْكَ لَهُ
وَأَشْهَدُ أَنَّ مُحَمَّدًا عَبْدُهُ وَرَسُوْلُهُ

I bear witness that there is no god but Allah alone;
He has no partner. And I bear witness that Muhammad is
Allah's servant and Messenger.

The Shahadah is made up of two parts:

1. The first part is about **Allah Almighty**

2. The second part is about **Prophet Muhammad** ﷺ

The Shahadah – Part One

Muslims believe that Allah is the One True God. There is no God other than Him. This is called **Tawhid**.

As Muslims, we believe:

- Allah is One; not two, three or more.

- Allah has no father or mother.

- Allah has no children.

- Allah made everything without any help from anyone or anything.

- Allah made everyone including our parents and family.

- Allah made the sun, moon, stars and everything in the universe.

- Allah made the rivers, seas and mountains.

- Allah made the trees, flowers and all the animals.

- Allah made everything in the whole world.

- Before anything was made, Allah was still there, and after everything has gone Allah will still be there.

- There was no god before Allah, and there will never be another god, ever.

- Allah is completely different to everything and everyone; He is not like us; He is not a man or a woman; He is not a boy or a girl; He is not young or old. Allah is so great that anything you can think of, or imagine, Allah is greater than that.

The Shahadah – Part Two

Muslims believe that Prophet Muhammad ﷺ is the Messenger of Allah. This is called **Risalah**.

Prophet Muhammad ﷺ was chosen by Allah, to be His Prophet and Messenger. Prophets and Messengers are special people sent by Allah to pass His message on to everyone else.

Allah sent many Prophets and Messengers before Prophet Muhammad ﷺ. Prophet Muhammad ﷺ is Allah's Last Prophet and Messenger. Allah will not send any Prophet or Messenger after him.

Prophet Muhammad ﷺ told everyone about Allah's message. This last message is known as the **Qur'an**.

Prophet Muhammad ﷺ is the person who told us about Allah. Without him, we would not know that Allah is the One and only God.

Prophet Nuh ﷺ –
The Great Flood

The children of Prophet Adam ﷺ travelled far and wide to the corners of the earth. No matter where they went, they were one big family, serving Allah and worshipping Him alone. As time passed, some people began to forget about the worship of Allah. Instead, they worshipped idols.

To guide the people, Allah decided to send a great Messenger. His name was Prophet Nuh ﷺ and he was a guide and a teacher. He spent his time reminding people about Allah. But the people did not pay attention to his message and made fun of him when he spoke and laughed at everything he had to say.

Very few people accepted the teachings of Prophet Nuh ﷺ, but Prophet Nuh ﷺ was very patient. He never stopped calling people to Allah. In fact, he continued in this way for 950 years!

Most people still did not listen. They continued to worship the idols.

Then one night, Allah sent a message to Prophet Nuh عليه السلام. He told him that He had finally decided to punish the disbelievers by sending a great flood. He commanded Prophet Nuh عليه السلام to build a huge boat, called an 'Ark'. Only those who believed would be able to go on it.

So Prophet Nuh عليه السلام did as he was commanded. He began to build the Ark, carrying pieces of wood and putting them together to build a huge ship. He was helped by the small group of people who believed in him. As for those people who did not believe him, this gave them more reason to make fun of him.

Nobody, except for the believers, could understand why he was building the Ark on dry land. Boats only float in water, they

thought, and there is no water here. Prophet Nuh ﷺ paid no attention to them. He finished the task and finally the great Ark was ready. Nobody had ever seen a ship of this size.

One last time, Prophet Nuh ﷺ turned to his people, and warned them, 'O my people! Very soon, Allah is going to punish you with a great flood. You, your families and everything you have will be destroyed by it. This is your last warning, so accept my call!'

The wicked people laughed at him. Prophet Nuh ﷺ and his small group of faithful followers then got on the Ark, and took with them animals, plants and seeds. They took food and everything else that they needed, and they waited.

Suddenly, the town fell silent. Everything was still. The people looked out of their houses, and saw dark black clouds gathering over the whole town. Strong winds began to blow, shaking the

trees, and rocking the Ark. And then, the first drops of rain began to fall.

The drops of rain became puddles, and the puddles became pools; and it rained, and rained, until the entire earth was under water. Even the mountains were covered by the water. All the disbelievers drowned, and the houses were all ruined. Only Prophet Nuh ﷺ and those on the Ark with him survived the storm.

Finally, after forty days and forty nights the rains stopped, and the storm went away. Not a single area of dry land was left on the earth. Then, after many days and nights had passed, a tiny rock appeared from under the water. It was the peak of a mountain; and one tiny rock at a time, the land began to reappear. Prophet Nuh ﷺ and his followers woke up to find that the Ark was no longer floating, and that the land had all dried up. They came out of the Ark in joy, and thanked Allah for keeping them safe.

Toilet Manners

Allah tells us in the Qur'an: *"Allah loves those who always turn to Him asking for forgiveness and He loves those who keep themselves well clean and pure."* (al-Baqara 2:222)

Du'a BEFORE Entering the Bathroom

اَللّٰهُمَّ إِنِّي أَعُوذُ بِكَ مِنَ الْخُبُثِ وَالْخَبَائِثِ

O Allah, I ask for Your protection from all dirt and unclean creatures.

Du'a AFTER Leaving the Bathroom

غُفْرَانَكَ. اَلْحَمْدُ لِلَّهِ الَّذِي أَذْهَبَ عَنِّي الْأَذٰى وَعَافَانِي

(O Allah,) I beg Your pardon. All Praise be to Allah, Who removed the difficulty from me and gave me ease.

The **Sunnah** is the way of Prophet Muhammad ﷺ. We follow the Sunnah because it is the best way to live our life. By following the Prophet's Sunnah, Allah will be happy with us.

The Prophet ﷺ taught us the following manners when using the toilet.

The Sunnah Manners of ENTERING the Bathroom:

1. Read the Du'a before entering.

2. Enter the bathroom with the left foot first.

3. Do not go in barefoot; use slippers that are only for the bathroom.

4. Take a lot of care to keep your clothes and body clean and dry. Gather your clothes and do not let them touch any dirt.

The Sunnah Manners while INSIDE the Bathroom:

1. Once you are inside, do not speak, sing or read anything; remain completely silent. You are only allowed to speak, if you are asking for help or need someone.

2. Always sit down to relieve yourself, never stand up. Be very careful about splashing any drops of urine.

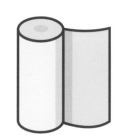

3. Make sure you are alone when you use the toilet, and that nobody sees you.

4. Stay sitting down for as long as you need the toilet and not any longer than that. Do not stay sitting on the toilet for no reason.

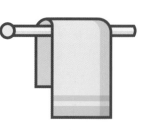

   Remember, the toilet is an unclean place and you must try and finish quickly and leave.

5. Once you have finished, clean yourself up. Perform **Istinja'**, using the left hand.

   Istinja' is to:

   - WIPE – Clean the dirty area using toilet paper.

   - WASH – Wash the dirty area with water.

   - WIPE – Wipe private parts dry with toilet paper.

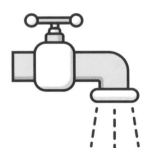

6. Flush the toilet and clean up after yourself. Make sure you clean the toilet and the toilet seat.

7. Clean the area around the toilet, if any water has been spilled or splashed.

8. Wash your hands very carefully using water and soap.

The Sunnah Manners of LEAVING the Bathroom:

1. Make sure your clothes are back on and you are fully covered before leaving.

2. Leave the bathroom with the right foot first.

3. When you are outside, read the Du'a of leaving the bathroom.

What to Say and When? (Part 2)

Planning for the Future:

When making a plan to do something for the future, we say '**In-shaa' Allah**' which means: 'If Allah so Wills'.

When Thanking Someone:

When we want to thank another Muslim, we say, '**Jazaa-kallaah**' which means: 'May Allah reward you'.

When someone says, '**Jazaa-kallaah**' to you, you should reply, '**Baara-kallahu feek**' which means: 'May Allah bless you'.

When We See Something We Like:

When we see or hear something nice and enjoyable we say, '*Maa shaa' Allah*' which means: 'This is Allah's wish'.

After Sneezing:

When someone sneezes they should say, '*Al-hamdu lillaah*', which means: 'All praise is for Allah'.

The one who hears somebody sneezing and saying '*Al-hamdu lillaah*' should say, '*Yarhamu-kallaah*', which means: 'May Allah have mercy on you'.

After this, the one who sneezed should say, '*Yahdee-kumullaah*', which means: 'May Allah guide you'.

The Sunnah Manners of Thanking:

Always thank people for anything they have done for you, gifts they have given you and even the small kind things people have done for you.

The Prophet ﷺ said, "Whoever does not thank people has not thanked Allah." (Ahmad)

Prophet Muhammad ﷺ taught us the different levels of showing thankfulness. They are:

o To do or give something which is the same back in return to the other person for the kindness that they showed you.

o To do or give something better back in return to the other person for the kindness that they showed you.

o If you cannot do one of the above two things, then at least pray for the person who showed you kindness or gave you a gift.

o Do not ignore or make fun of any kindness that is shown to you.

o   Do not reject gifts.

o   Do not take back a gift that you have given to someone else.

The Sunnah Manners of Sneezing:

o Cover your mouth when you sneeze. This should be done with a tissue or handkerchief. If you do not have one, then use your hands.

o Do not sneeze towards another person.

o After sneezing clean your nose and mouth, and then say the words mentioned earlier.

Sirah: The Story of the Elephants

Once upon a time, in Yemen, there lived a ruler called Abrahah al-Ashram. He built a great church in an area called Sana`a and he wanted all the people to come to it.

He had seen how the people of Arabia visited the Ka`bah, which was built by Prophet Ibrahim ﷺ and Prophet Isma`il ﷺ. The Ka`bah was a very important place even at that time for the people of Arabia, because it was the house of Allah; they would visit it every year to worship there.

After Abrahah built the church, he called the people to visit it. He believed that everyone would stop visiting the Ka`bah and only come to his church, but this did not happen.

Abrahah saw that people were not coming to his church. This made Abrahah very angry and he decided to destroy the Ka`bah so that everyone would come to his church only. He got his army together, which included many soldiers and large elephants, and he set off to Makkah to destroy the House of Allah.

`Abdul Muttalib, who was Prophet Muhammad's grandfather, called all the people together. They prayed to Allah to protect the Ka`bah and to help them against Abrahah and his army. They then left Makkah with their families and went to some hills to see what would happen.

Abrahah ordered his army to move towards Makkah, but the elephants would not move! The soldiers tried their best to make the elephants stand up; they hit the elephants with iron sticks and poked their bellies, but nothing happened. The elephants stayed sitting like rocks. They then turned the elephants in the direction away from

Makkah, and the elephants got up and moved. The elephants would move in every direction except towards Makkah!

When Abrahah was trying to move the elephants, the sky suddenly went dark. A big group of birds were flying towards them. Every bird was carrying three small stones; one in its beak and two in its feet. The birds dropped the small stones on the soldiers and killed them all.

Abrahah was badly hurt. He got scared and fled from Makkah. When he reached Yemen, he died from his injuries. Allah destroyed his army and protected the Ka`bah. `Abdul Muttalib and the people of Makkah returned to their homes and they thanked Allah for helping them against Abrahah.

The people were so happy. They called the Quraysh the 'People of Allah' because Allah listened to their prayer. Quraysh is the tribe that Prophet Muhammad ﷺ belonged too.

A wise man from the people said that this was a sign from Allah that a greater blessing is about to come, and he was right. This year was known as the 'Year of the Elephants', and it was in this year that our Beloved Prophet Muhammad ﷺ was born.

The Rules of Wudu'

A Muslim who is not clean cannot pray Salah, do the Tawaf or touch the Holy Qur'an. Prophet Muhammad ﷺ said, "Whoever is not clean, has no prayer." (at-Tabarani)

To become clean and be able to read and touch the Holy Qur'an, we have to do Wudu'. Wudu' is a special way of washing ourselves that gets us ready for reading the Salah and the Qur'an.

We perform Wudu' in the following manner:

1. Make intention in your heart to perform Wudu'.

2. Say: Bismillaahir Rahmaanir Raheem.

Three times

3. Wash hands to wrists three times. Pass the fingers of the two hands in between each other.

Three times

4. Rinse mouth three times. Use your right hand. You can use a miswaak/toothbrush to clean your teeth.

Three times

5. Rinse nose three times. Use your right hand to sniff the water and your left hand to clean your nose.

Three times

6. Wash face three times. Make sure to include all parts of your face from the top of your forehead to your chin and from one earlobe to the next. Make sure no part of the skin is left dry.

Three times

7. Wash right arm first, then left arm three times each. Make sure to include your elbows.

Once

8. Wipe the head by passing wet hands over it; front to back once. Wet your hands with unused water and use your last three fingers and palm to wipe over.

Once

9. Wipe the ears; inside and out once. From the same wet hands, now use your index finger and thumb.

Once

10. Wipe the back of the neck once. From the same wet hands, use the back of your hand.

Three times

11. Wash right foot first then left foot three times each. Make sure to include your ankles and to wash in between your toes.

12. Recite the Shahadah and the Du`a after Wudu'.

The Shahadah

أَشْهَدُ أَنْ لَّا إِلَهَ إِلَّا اللهُ وَحْدَهُ لَا شَرِيكَ لَهُ
وَأَشْهَدُ أَنَّ مُحَمَّدًا عَبْدُهُ وَرَسُوْلُهُ

I bear witness that there is no god but Allah alone;
He has no partner. And I bear witness that Muhammad is
Allah's servant and Messenger.

(Muslim)

Du'a After Wudu'

اَللّٰهُمَّ اجْعَلْنِي مِنَ التَّوَّابِيْنَ وَاجْعَلْنِي مِنَ الْمُتَطَهِّرِيْنَ

O Allah! Make me from those who repent and make me
from those who are clean.

(at-Tirmidhi)

What BREAKS the Wudu':

Going to
the toilet

Passing wind (even if
we do it by accident)

Sleeping

Vomiting

Bleeding

Some Rulings on the Wudu':

In the Wudu', there are actions that are obligatory (Fard),
recommended (Sunnah) and disliked (Makruh).

The **obligatory (Fard)** actions for Wudu' are:

1. Washing the face

2. Washing the hands and arms up to and including the
    elbow

3. Wiping one-quarter of the head

4. Washing the feet up to and including the ankles

Examples of the recommended (Sunnah) actions in the Wudu' are:

1. Making an intention (niyyah) to perform the Wudu'

2. Saying the Tasmiyah (Bismillaah)

3. Brushing the teeth

4. Rinsing the mouth and nose

5. Wiping the ears and the back of the neck

6. Washing two or three times

7. Starting from the right side first

8. Washing the body continuously without a break

9. Washing the body in the correct order

10. Rubbing the skin while washing

Examples of the disliked (Makruh) actions in the Wudu' are:

1. Using too much water or wasting it

2. Using too less water

3. Striking the face with the water

4. Speaking to others during Wudu'

When we perform the Wudu' it is **recommended (Mustahabb)** to say the following prayers:

*   When rinsing the **mouth,** pray that Allah gives you the ability to read the Qur'an.

*   When rinsing the **nose,** pray that Allah protects you from the smell of the Hellfire and grants you the scent of Paradise.

*   When washing the **face,** pray that Allah brightens your face on the Day of Judgement

*   When washing the **arms,** pray that Allah grants you your book of deeds in the right hand and not in the left hand.

*   When wiping the **head,** pray that Allah shades you under the shade of His `Arsh (Throne) on the Day of Judgement.

*   When washing the **feet,** pray that Allah gives you firmness on the Sirat (bridge over Hell) and that you do not slip.

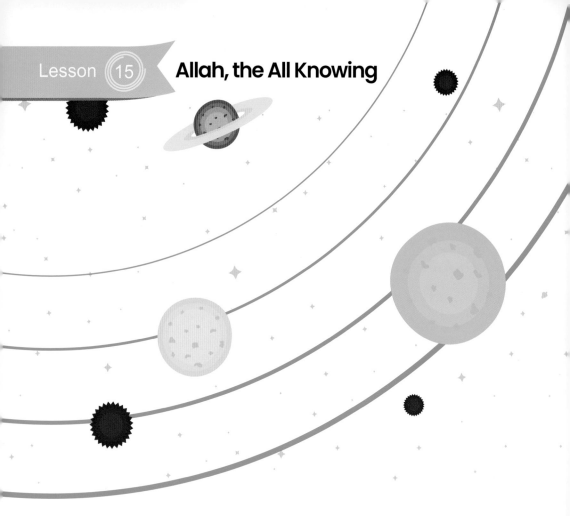

Allah, the All Knowing

As Muslims, we believe that Allah Almighty is **All-Knowing** and **All-Aware**. This means that He knows everything, whether we can see it or not. No matter how big or how small something is, it is known to Allah. He knows the feelings in our hearts and the thoughts in our minds. Allah knows everything that we do and say; out in front of everyone and our hidden secrets.

Two of the Beautiful Names of Allah are **al-`Alim** (The All-Knowing) and **al-Khabir** (The Ever-Aware)

From the tiniest ant in the forest, to the fish at the bottom of the deep sea, Allah knows everything about them. He knows where a tree will grow, where its leaves will fall and who will eat the fruit from the tree. Allah's knowledge is so great that it can not be measured.

Allah is All-Seeing and All-Hearing. He sees and hears everything. He knows what has happened in the past and He knows what will happen in the future.

Allah knows everything that we do. On the Day of Judgement, He will tell us what we did, and if we were good we will go to Paradise (Jannah) and if we were bad we will go to Hell (Jahannum).

The Qur'an tells us:

- Allah knows everything that is in the heavens and everything that is in the earth. He has complete and perfect knowledge of all things.

- Allah knows what we speak out aloud and He also knows all our hidden secrets.

- Allah knows what is in the land and in the sea. And not a leaf falls without Him knowing about it. There is not a grain in any part of the earth, or anything green or dry that is not recorded by Allah. Everything is known and recorded by Allah.

- Allah is the Knower of the things that we see and the things that we cannot see. He is the Greatest, the Most-High.

Prophet Ibrahim عليه السلام (Part 1) - The Broken Idols

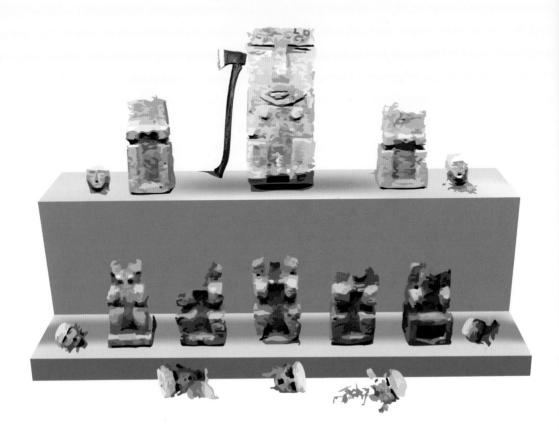

Prophet Ibrahim عليه السلام was born in Iraq, many thousands of years ago. Allah had chosen him to be His Prophet and Messenger, to guide his people to the worship of the One True God.

As a child, Prophet Ibrahim عليه السلام would look around the world and think about the creation of Allah. At that time the people believed that things like the stars and the moon were gods. Prophet Ibrahim عليه السلام wanted to teach the people about Allah, because he wanted his people to worship Allah alone, and not make any partners with Him.

One night, when Prophet Ibrahim ﷺ was with the people, he saw a great star in the night sky. "Is this my Lord?" he said.

But when the night passed, and the star could not be seen any longer, he said, "This cannot be my Lord."

Then, later, he saw the full moon shining brightly, and he said to the people, "Is this my Lord?"

But when the first light of morning spread across the sky, and the moon could not be seen anymore, he said, "If my Lord had not guided me, I would have been like you; I would have gone on the wrong path."

Then the sun rose high in the sky, and it covered all the lands with its heat and light, and so Prophet Ibrahim ﷺ speaking to the people said, "Is this my Lord? This one is the biggest."

But as the hours went by, the sun's light started to dim, and the heat of the sun lessened, until the sun set and could not be seen anymore. Speaking to his people, Prophet Ibrahim ﷺ said, "My people! I do not worship what you worship other than Allah."

This is how Prophet Ibrahim ﷺ taught his people about Allah. The stars, sun and moon are all Allah's signs and they are His creation. They are not His partners or anything that should be worshipped besides Him. Allah never fades away or becomes weak; He is the All-Powerful and the One Who looks after us all.

One day, Prophet Ibrahim ﷺ saw his uncle Azar make idols and statues out of wood and stone. Azar would sell these idols to people, and they would worship them and take them as gods other than Allah.

Prophet Ibrahim ﷺ asked his uncle Azar about this, but Azar got angry and told Prophet Ibrahim ﷺ not to say anything against the idols. Instead, Prophet Ibrahim ﷺ prayed for his uncle that Allah guides him to the truth.

Prophet Ibrahim ﷺ was surprised with his people. How could they worship these idols and statues when they could not help or harm anyone? They could not even help themselves. But still the people took these objects as gods beside Allah, believing that they were the reason for all the good things they received in their life.

When Prophet Ibrahim ﷺ asked his people why they worship these idols, they had no answer, except to say that this is how their fathers and their

fathers before them would worship. So, Prophet Ibrahim ﷺ thought of a plan to show them the reality of these idols, so that they could see the truth.

One night, when the people went out to celebrate on the day of their festival, Prophet Ibrahim ﷺ decided to stay back. The people asked him to come with them, but he told them that he was sick and that he could not go. So, they went without him.

When the people left, Prophet Ibrahim ﷺ went to the temple where all the statues and idols were kept. He went up to the idols and asked them, "Do you not eat? What is the matter with you that you do not speak?"

He then slowly took an axe in his right hand and began to break the idols one by one. He broke them all except for the biggest one from all of them. He put the axe around the biggest idol's neck and then he left.

As the people came back from their festival, they found their idols broken and smashed into pieces, except for the big idol. They were angered by this and wanted to know who did it. They remembered Prophet Ibrahim ﷺ, and they believed that he had something to do with this because he used to speak against their false gods.

The people went to Prophet Ibrahim ﷺ and asked him, "Did you do this to our gods, O Ibrahim?"

Prophet Ibrahim ﷺ replied, "He did it – the big one. Ask them, if they can speak."

The people looked to themselves, knowing that they were in the wrong. They said to Prophet Ibrahim ﷺ, "You know that they cannot speak."

Prophet Ibrahim ﷺ then turned to them and said, "Do you worship besides Allah something that cannot bring you any help or harm? Shame on you and these idols that you worship besides Allah. Do you not have any sense?"

The people were silenced, because they knew that they were in the wrong, and Prophet Ibrahim ﷺ was right, but they did not want to accept what Prophet Ibrahim ﷺ was saying. Their hearts and minds were closed to the truth and they were unable to understand that their actions were wrong.

Prophet Ibrahim ﷺ (Part 2) – The Great Fire

Upon returning from their festival, the people found their idols smashed and broken into pieces. They knew Prophet Ibrahim ﷺ must have been behind this, as he stayed behind and did not take part in their festivities. When the people asked Prophet Ibrahim ﷺ if he did it, he told them to ask the idols what had happened, but the people knew they were only wood and stone and that they could not speak.

The people understood that they were in the wrong, but their hearts were sealed to the truth. Instead of admitting they were in the wrong, they became even more arrogant and moved further away from the truth. They wanted to punish Prophet Ibrahim ﷺ for showing how foolish they were. As they were thinking of what to do, they came up with the idea to throw Prophet Ibrahim ﷺ in a great fire. "Burn him and help your gods!" they said to one another.

The people began to collect lots of firewood from everywhere. They thought that their gods would be happy with them for doing this. The people kept on collecting the firewood as the days went by until the fire became so huge that nothing like it had ever been seen before. The fire was so hot that no one could go near it, without getting burnt. It looked as though the sparks from the fire would touch the sky.

The people tied Prophet Ibrahim's hands behind his back and put him in a catapult and then threw him into the fire. As Prophet Ibrahim ﷺ was falling into the fire, Angel Jibra'il came to him and said, "O Ibrahim! Is there anything you need?" Prophet Ibrahim ﷺ said, "From you, no!"

Prophet Ibrahim ﷺ had trust in Allah and only asked Allah to protect him. The angel of rain came and asked him if he should release the rain and put out the fire. But Prophet Ibrahim ﷺ did not accept his offer and kept on saying, "Allah is enough for us and an excellent protector He is."

When Prophet Ibrahim ﷺ was thrown into the fire, Allah ordered the fire to be cool for him and not to hurt him. The fire

did as Allah commanded it and it was cool like a garden for Prophet Ibrahim ﷺ, who enjoyed his days and nights in it.

When the people saw that the fire did not harm Prophet Ibrahim ﷺ, they were shocked, and they knew Prophet Ibrahim ﷺ was telling the truth, but they still did not want to believe in his message. Prophet Ibrahim ﷺ came out of the fire without being harmed and he was safe and sound. This is how Allah helps those who believe in him.

The people failed to defeat Prophet Ibrahim ﷺ and their plan to burn him in the great fire did not work. The King of Babylon, Nimrud, heard about this great miracle so he called Prophet Ibrahim ﷺ to question him. He wanted to know why he did not worship him and their false gods.

The king asked, "Who is your Lord?"

"My Lord is the One Who gives life and death," Prophet Ibrahim ﷺ replied.

"I give life and death," said the king. He then brought two prisoners. Previously, the king had ordered one of the prisoners to be killed and the other to be freed, but he changed his mind. He now ordered the one to be freed to be killed instead, and the one to be killed to be freed. In this way, he falsely believed that he was the one who gave life and death.

Seeing how foolish the king was, Prophet Ibrahim ﷺ said, "My Lord is He Who makes the sun rise from the east, so why don't you make it rise from the west."

When the king heard this, he became speechless. He did not reply to this, nor did he want to believe in Prophet Ibrahim ﷺ and accept the One True God, Allah. Instead, he ordered Prophet Ibrahim ﷺ to leave Iraq and not to return.

Sirah: The Birth of the Prophet ﷺ

Almost 1500 years ago, Allah, through His Kindness, blessed the people of Arabia. The Arabs had forgotten the right way of their forefather Prophet Ibrahim ﷺ and had started worshipping idols instead of worshipping Allah, Most High.

Although they had many good qualities, the Arabs were far away from Allah's guidance, and that is why they had many bad habits. They harmed women, buried their daughters alive and treated the weak people in a very bad way.

They were known for fighting over silly things like who owned a water well, or land, and sometimes, even over the results of a camel race! They gambled, drank alcohol, had fights and wasted their money. All this was because they did not follow the teachings of Allah.

It was at this time that Allah blessed the Arabs. The arrival of Allah's most beloved Prophet ﷺ, who is the greatest blessing of Allah, was near. The Prophet's grandfather, `Abdul Muttalib, was told by many good people that his grandson would grow up to be a great person. So `Abdul Muttalib began to think of a name for his grandson.

He thought hard about this for six days, but he still could not decide what the child's name should be. On the seventh day, as he thought once again about a name for the baby, he suddenly felt sleepy. In a dream, he heard a voice instructing him that the baby must be named MUHAMMAD, which means, 'The Most Praised One'.

Surprised by the voice in his dream, he woke up and rushed to Prophet Muhammad's mother, Lady Aminah, to tell her about the name. As he informed her, she smiled and told him that she had seen the very same dream and had been given the very same instructions.

One bright Meccan night, the sky was lit up from the east to the west. There was a special glow covering the entire city and a warm feeling filled the air. What was going on? This was a night unlike any other. Something special was about to happen.

As the travellers went to their tents for the night, they saw that the heavens were glowing, as though the stars had come down closer to the earth. That night, all the animals on the earth could speak. The desert rabbits, camels, wolves and all the other creatures of the earth were able to talk and understand each other. Together, they sang songs praising Allah and spoke of the birth of the last Prophet, the leader of all Prophets and the best of Allah's creation ﷺ.

In the early hours of a blessed Monday morning, the 12th of Rabi' al-Awwal, Lady Aminah had her baby. The special Light that had been passed down from generation to generation throughout the years was now shining from Lady Aminah. The Light was so bright that she saw the valleys and palaces of Bosra in Syria.

As the dazzling light in her room lowered, Lady Aminah's eyes met with the most beautiful baby ever born; her son, whom she named **Muhammad**. As she looked at the beauty

of the baby in wonder, the baby raised himself up and said, "There is no God but Allah, and I am His Prophet." The little baby Muhammad then fell into prostration and worshipped Allah. A musical voice then filled the room, saying, "May peace be upon you, O Prophet, and Allah's mercy and His kindest blessings."

Lady Aminah then sent news of the Prophet's birth to his grandfather, `Abdul Muttalib. When he heard the news, he was so happy that he took the baby in his arms and rushed out towards the Ka`bah. `Abdul Muttalib circled the Ka`bah seven times, holding the baby, and then announced that he had been gifted with a grandchild, and his name was Muhammad.

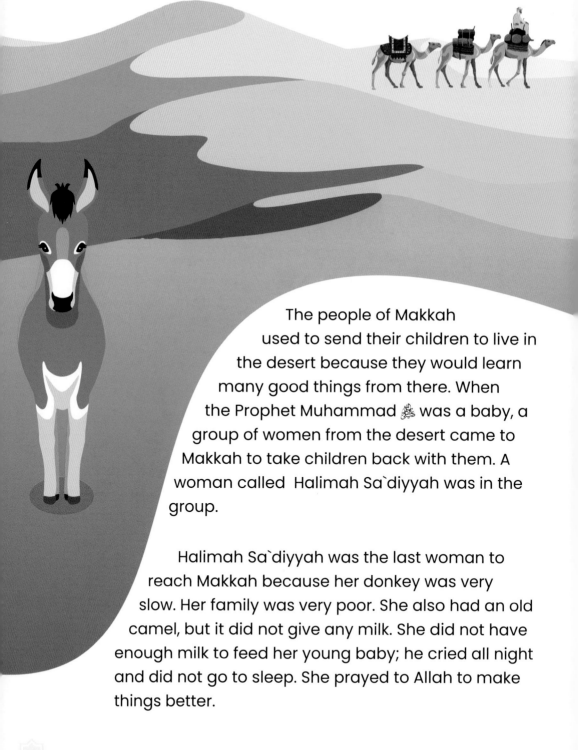

Sirah: Halimah Sa`diyyah

The people of Makkah used to send their children to live in the desert because they would learn many good things from there. When the Prophet Muhammad ﷺ was a baby, a group of women from the desert came to Makkah to take children back with them. A woman called Halimah Sa`diyyah was in the group.

Halimah Sa`diyyah was the last woman to reach Makkah because her donkey was very slow. Her family was very poor. She also had an old camel, but it did not give any milk. She did not have enough milk to feed her young baby; he cried all night and did not go to sleep. She prayed to Allah to make things better.

When she came to Makkah, she saw Prophet Muhammad ﷺ who was an orphan child (orphan means that his father had died). The other women did not want to look after an orphan. They said, "We expect a reward from the child's father. What can the mother of the child do for us?" All the other women found children to take back with them, but Halimah Sa`diyyah could not find any.

Before leaving she said to her husband, al-Harith, "I do not want to go back to my friends and not have a baby to look after. Let's take the orphan baby."

"Yes, maybe Allah will give us blessings because of it." Al-Harith replied.

So, Halimah Sa`diyyah took Prophet Muhammad ﷺ with her.

When she came to Makkah, her donkey was the slowest, but on the way back home her donkey was the fastest. Her friends were surprised and asked Halimah, "Is this the same donkey as before?"

Halimah said, "Yes, it is."

"What a lovely surprise!" They said.

On the first day, she gave Prophet Muhammad ﷺ milk to drink, and he drank until he was full. Then she gave her young son milk to drink, and he drank until he was full.

Then al-Harith went to the old camel to get some milk, and he saw that the camel gave so much milk that he and Halimah Sa`diyyah drank until they were full. That night when they went to bed they had a good night's sleep. When they woke up, al-Harith said to Halimah Sa`diyyah, "We have never had a better night than this before."

Many good things started to happen to Halimah Sa'diyyah because of Prophet Muhammad ﷺ.

When Halimah Sa'diyyah got home, she saw that there was not much grass for the animals to eat because there had been no rain for the grass to grow.

So, Halimah Sa'diyyah sent her goats and camels to the fields where there was more grass so that they could eat there. Her animals ate until they were full, and they came back home filled with lots of milk.

The other people in the village saw this, and they sent their animals to graze there as well, but their animals were still hungry and empty of milk when they came back.

They soon realised that Halimah Sa'diyyah enjoyed these good things only because she was looking after Prophet Muhammad ﷺ.

Eating Manners

Food and drink are great blessings from Allah. It is important that we pay careful attention to our food and drink because Allah has given us our bodies to look after and protect.

   Prophet Muhammad ﷺ told us that we need to look after our bodies. We need to eat good, healthy food, so that our bodies become strong and we are able to do things.

   It is very important that we use the blessing of food in ways that makes Allah happy, and we need to make sure that we do not disrespect food by wasting it or eating too much.

The Sunnah Manners BEFORE Eating

1.   Wash your hands carefully.

2.   Eat with the intention of making your body strong so that you can worship Allah and do good deeds.

3.   Sit down to eat; do not eat when you are standing/walking/playing.

4. Do not eat whilst doing other things, such as playing or watching TV, etc.

5. Try to eat with other people like your family or friends.

6. Recite the Du'a before eating, asking Allah to bless the food and make you stronger by eating it.

The Sunnah Manners WHILE Eating

1. Eat with the right hand.

2. Stay sitting down until the food is finished.

3. Chew the food well before swallowing it.

4. Do not eat too quickly.

5. Do not talk with your mouth full of food.

6. Do not open your mouth in a way that shows the food.

7. Eat the food that is nearest to you.

8. Do not sniff the food.

9. Do not blow on the food.

10. Do not waste the food by throwing it away.

11. Do not eat too much food so that you feel sick or your tummy hurts.

Du'a BEFORE Eating

بِسْمِ اللّٰهِ وَعَلَى بَرَكَةِ اللّٰهِ

(I begin) in the Name of Allah and by Allah's blessings.

Du'a AFTER Eating

اَلْحَمْدُ لِلّٰهِ الَّذِيْ أَطْعَمَنَا وَسَقَانَا وَجَعَلَنَا مِنَ الْمُسْلِمِيْنَ

All praise is for Allah Who gave us food and drink,
and Who made us Muslims.

12. Do not fill your plate too much; start with a small size of food that you know you will finish. You can always ask for more after you have finished.

13. Try your best not to make a mess on your plate, the table or your clothes. Be as clean as you can and be careful of not touching something clean if your hands are messy.

14. Thank Allah in your heart for every bite of food that you eat.

The Sunnah Manners AFTER Eating

1. Recite the Du`a after eating when you have finished your food.

2. Wash your hands well. Make sure that you get rid of bits of food and the smell of the food from your hands.

3. Rinse your mouth and get rid of any food bits in your mouth and between your teeth.

The Second Pillar of Islam: Salah

Salah is the second pillar of Islam. Salah is the Arabic word for Prayer. We pray to Allah five times, each day, at different times of the day.

1. FAJR – This is the Dawn Prayer, which we pray in the morning before the sun comes out.

2. ZUHR – This is the Early Afternoon Prayer, which we pray after midday.

3. `ASR – This is the Late Afternoon Prayer, which we pray a short time before sunset.

4. MAGHRIB – The Evening prayer, which we pray straight after the sun has set.

5. `ISHA' – The Night Prayer, which we pray from when Maghrib ends, until Fajr starts the next day.

As Muslims, prayer is the most important activity of our everyday lives. We should always make time for the five daily prayers. The five daily prayers make our lives special and blessed.

The Salah is an appointment that we have every day with Allah Almighty that we must keep. It is important to keep our appointments with other people; it is much more important to keep them with Allah. Salah gives us a chance every day to stand in front of Allah, worship Him, speak with Him, and tell Him how much we love Him.

The purpose of the Salah is to fully concentrate and give your full attention to Allah and His remembrance. During Salah, we must try our hardest not to think about things that will stop us from thinking about Allah. Allah commands us in the Qur'an, *"Perform the prayers to remember Me alone."* (Taha 20:14)

Salah is a powerful good deed. It takes away all the bad deeds that you might have done between the prayers. So, when you pray the Zuhr prayer, all the bad things you might have accidentally done from Fajr to Zuhr will be completely removed; they are taken out of your Book of Deeds.

There is a very special way that the Salah is performed. We were told about this special way by Prophet Muhammad ﷺ, who said to his Companions, "Pray (exactly) as you see me pray." Since the Prophet ﷺ is the most perfect human being and his prayer is the most perfect, we must try our best to make our prayer the same as his prayer, as much as we can.

Sirah: Meeting Bahirah, the Monk

When Prophet Muhammad ﷺ was four years old, he returned to the loving care of his mother, Lady Aminah. He remained with her till she passed away when he was six years of age.

At such a young and tender age, Prophet Muhammad ﷺ lost both of his parents, and was taken into the care of his noble grandfather `Abdul Muttalib. But two years had not passed when `Abdul Muttalib also passed away, leaving the Prophet ﷺ in the loving care of his uncle Abu Talib.

Abu Talib would love Prophet Muhammad ﷺ like his own children. He took great care of him and always kept him close to him. Whenever he would go on a journey, he would always take his young nephew along with him. When the Prophet ﷺ was twelve years old, Abu Talib took him on his business trip to a country called Syria.

When they were passing a small town called Bosra, in Syria, a Christian monk called Bahirah stopped them and invited them for a meal. Bahirah lived in a monastery, which is a

place where monks stay all day and night and do not have any contact with the outside world. Abu Talib had passed Bahirah's monastery many times on his journeys, but they had never been invited inside by him before.

This time when Bahirah saw the group of people with Abu Talib, he noticed something different. He saw a cloud in the sky which was giving shade to the group and protecting it from the sun, and when they sat next to a tree the tree lowered its branches to also give shade from the sun.

Bahirah had the most knowledge from all of the monks of his time and he knew a lot of things. He had all the holy books with him, which he got from his teachers. In these books he had read about the signs of when another prophet will come, and he knew from these signs that the Prophet they were waiting for was part of this group of people. This is why he invited the whole group to the monastery, adults and children, and ordered them to not leave anyone behind.

The group accepted the invitation, but they left Prophet Muhammad ﷺ behind to look after their things, because he was the youngest person in the group. As they were eating, Bahirah looked at every one of them, but he could not see the Prophet ﷺ. He asked if they had left anyone behind. They replied, "No one stayed behind except a young boy who is looking after our things." Bahirah said, "No, you must also bring him to eat as well."

When the Prophet ﷺ came, Bahirah looked at him clearly and saw all the signs of the coming Prophet in him. As the meal ended, Bahirah got up and said to Prophet Muhammad ﷺ, "Young man! I want to ask you something by al-Lat and al-ʿUzza, will you answer me?" (al-Lat and al-ʿUzza were the names of the idols that the Arabs used to worship).

Bahirah only said the names of the idols because he had heard the Arab people say this. When the Prophet ﷺ heard these words, he said to Bahirah, "Do not ask me anything by al-Lat and al-ʿUzza. By Allah, nothing is more hated to me than them."

Bahirah then asked Prophet Muhammad ﷺ questions about his life, his habits and tastes. As the Prophet ﷺ was replying to his questions, Bahirah could see all the signs of the expected prophet in him. He then looked at the Prophet's back and saw the 'Seal of Prophethood' between his shoulders, which was the shape of a pigeon's egg.

Seeing these signs, Bahirah knew that Prophet Muhammad ﷺ was definitely the Prophet of God. He turned to Abu Talib and asked him, "How is this boy related to you?"

"He is my son," Abu Talib replied.

"He cannot be your son," Bahirah told him. "His father cannot be alive."

"He is my brother's son," said Abu Talib.

"So, what happened to his father?" asked Bahirah.

"He died," Abu Talib replied, "before Muhammad was born."

"You have spoken the truth," Bahirah said. "Take your nephew back home with you and be careful of the Arab Jews because if they see him and they recognise the signs I have seen, they will want to hurt him. So, hurry up and go back to your city. Your nephew definitely has a great future in front of him."

The Names of the Great Prophets

Prophets and Messengers were sent to all nations and to different parts of the world. It is related that there were roughly 124,000 Prophets and 313 Messengers, but the true number is only known by Allah.

From the thousands of Prophets, 25 of the greatest Prophets have been mentioned in the Qur'an. The first of them was Prophet Adam ﷺ and the last was Prophet Muhammad ﷺ.

Some of the Prophets are also mentioned in other holy books, such as the Bible. The 25 Prophets mentioned in the Qur'an are mentioned below, with their biblical names.

01 Adam (Adam) ﷺ

The father of all the people, and the first human being and Prophet sent by Allah.

02 Idris (Enoch) ﷺ

The great-grandfather of Prophet Nuh ﷺ.

03 Nuh (Noah) ﷺ

The Prophet who built the Ark. He called his people to the worship of Allah for 950 years.

04 Hud (Eber) ﷺ

The Ancient Arabian Prophet who was sent to `Ad. His people refused to believe in him, so they were punished with a sandstorm.

05 Salih (Shelah) ﷺ

The Prophet sent to Thamud. He was given a camel as a sign, but some of his people killed it so they were punished.

06 Ibrahim (Abraham) ﷺ

The Prophet who broke the idols and was thrown into the Great Fire, which Allah made cool for him.

07 Lut (Lot) ﷺ

The nephew of Prophet Ibrahim ﷺ. He was sent to a wicked people who were destroyed by a volcanic eruption because they refused to give up their evil practices.

08 Isma`il (Ishmael) ﷺ

The elder son of Prophet Ibrahim ﷺ. He helped his father build the Ka`bah, and his mother Hajar (Hagar) was gifted the Zamzam.

09 Ishaq (Isaac) ﷺ

The younger son of Prophet Ibrahim ﷺ and the father of Prophet Ya`qub.

10   Ya'qub (Jacob) ﷺ

The father of Prophet Yusuf ﷺ. The Bani Isra'il were his children.

11   Yusuf (Joseph) ﷺ

The Prophet who was thrown into the well by his brothers and who then became the governor of Egypt.

12   Ayyub (Job) ﷺ

The Prophet who showed great patience through difficulty and sickness. He was a true and devout servant of Allah.

13 Shu'ayb (Jethro) ﷺ

The Prophet sent to Madyan to the people of Ayka, who worshipped trees.

14 Harun (Aaron) ﷺ

The brother of Prophet Musa ﷺ.

15 Musa (Moses) ﷺ

The Prophet sent to challenge Pharaoh and who led the Bani Isra'il out of Egypt.

16

Al-Yasa (Elisha) ﷺ

A great Prophet of Bani Isra'il.

17

Dhu al-Kifl (Ezekiel) ﷺ

A great Prophet of Bani Isra'il.

18

Dawud (David) ﷺ

The father of Prophet Sulayman ﷺ and one of the kings of the Bani Isra'il. He defeated Jalut (Goliath).

19

Sulayman (Solomon) ﷺ

The Prophet who was a great king. He commanded the winds and could understand the speech of birds and what the animals would say.

20

Ilyas (Elija) ﷺ

A great Prophet of Bani Isra'il.

21

Yunus (Jonah) ﷺ

The Prophet who was swallowed by a whale. He was sent to the people of Nineveh in Iraq.

22   Zakariyya (Zacharias) ﷺ

The Prophet who looked after Lady Maryam, the Mother of Prophet `Isa ﷺ.

23   Yahya (John, the Baptist) ﷺ

The son of Prophet Zakariyya ﷺ and the cousin of Prophet `Isa ﷺ. A great Prophet of Bani Isra'il.

24   `Isa (Jesus) ﷺ

The Prophet who spoke from the cradle and was raised to the heavens.

25 Muhammad ﷺ

The beloved of Allah and the leader of all the Prophets.

Prophet Muhammad ﷺ is the **last** Prophet of Allah. All the Prophets were sent for a single people or tribe, but Prophet Muhammad ﷺ was sent to the whole of humankind. He is the Prophet for people of every race and colour, and no prophet will be born after him.

Prophet Musa ﷺ (Part 1) — Early Life and Miracles

The fortune-tellers told Pharaoh that a child would be born among the children of Israel, and this child would bring an end to his kingdom. Pharaoh did not want this to happen, so he ordered his soldiers to kill all the new baby boys born to the Bani Isra'il. During that year, Prophet Musa ﷺ was born.

Prophet Musa's mother was worried for her baby, because she knew Pharaoh would kill him. Allah told Prophet Musa's mother not to worry because He would look after him. He ordered her to put Prophet Musa ﷺ in a basket and to put him in the River Nile. So, Prophet Musa's mother did this. She had trust in Allah and knew He would look after Prophet Musa ﷺ.

The basket kept on sailing down the River Nile until it reached Pharaoh's palace. When the basket neared the palace, it was found by Asiyah, who was Pharaoh's wife. She opened the basket and found a beautiful baby boy inside it. She was so happy to see Prophet Musa ﷺ and decided to keep him and adopt him as her son. She convinced the Pharaoh to keep him and not to kill him.

Prophet Musa ﷺ grew up in Pharaoh's palace. He grew up to be a very tall and strong man. One day, when he went out of the palace, he saw two men fighting; one man was from Pharaoh's people and the other man was from the Bani Isra'il. The man from Bani Isra'il called out and asked Prophet Musa ﷺ to help him. So, Prophet Musa ﷺ tried to help him. As he was helping him, he pushed back the man from Pharaoh's people and accidently killed him.

On the next day, Prophet Musa ﷺ saw the same man from the Bani Isra'il fighting again with another person from Pharaoh's people. The man called out to Prophet Musa ﷺ again to help him. Prophet Musa ﷺ saw that the man from the Bani Isra'il was creating trouble and he got angry at him. The man got scared and said, "Are you going to kill me like the way you killed the other man yesterday?"

The news spread that it was Prophet Musa ﷺ who killed the man from Pharaoh's people. Someone who cared for Prophet Musa ﷺ told him to go far away from Egypt, because Pharaoh had ordered his soldiers to find him and to kill him. Prophet Musa ﷺ got worried. He decided to leave Egypt and find another place to live.

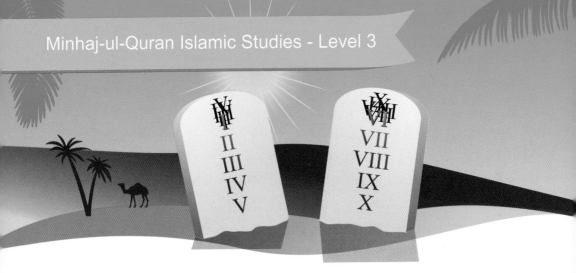

Prophet Musa ﷺ travelled to a place called Madyan. When he reached there, he took some rest. As he was resting, he saw some people approaching with their herd of goats and they started taking water out of the well. They gave their herd of goats water to drink. There were two young girls who were unable to get water, so Prophet Musa ﷺ got up to help them and took out the water from the well and gave it to them.

The girls told their father about Prophet Musa ﷺ helping them, so he decided to invite him over to talk. The father offered to get Prophet Musa ﷺ married to one of his daughters, if he helped him with his work for eight years, because he was an old man. Prophet Musa ﷺ agreed to this, and after fulfilling his promise he got married to the old man's daughter.

After ten years had passed, Prophet Musa ﷺ decided to return to Egypt with his family. On his way travelling back to Egypt, he wanted to light a fire because the night was very dark and cold, but Prophet Musa ﷺ could not find anything to make a fire with. However, he saw a fire in the distance and he told his family to stay where they were so that he may bring back some of the fire.

When Prophet Musa ﷺ reached the fire, he found a burning tree. He was called by a voice that said, "O Musa! I am your Lord, so take off your shoes; surely you are in the sacred valley of Tuwa! And I have chosen you, so listen to what I have revealed."

Prophet Musa ﷺ removed his shoes. He saw the fire was getting brighter and the tree was turning greener. Allah ordered Prophet Musa ﷺ to throw his staff (stick) on the ground. When Prophet Musa ﷺ did this, he saw that it had turned into a very big snake. He was afraid of it, but Allah told him not to worry. When he touched the snake, it turned back into a staff again. Allah then ordered him to put his hand in his pocket and to take it out, and when he did that he saw that his hand was shining bright.

Prophet Musa ﷺ (Part 2) Challenging Pharaoh

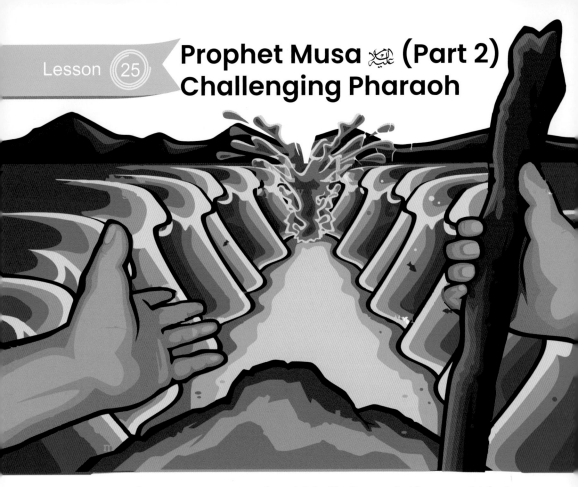

When Prophet Musa ﷺ received his first revelation and his two miracles at the sacred valley of Tuwa, Allah commanded him to go to Pharaoh and tell him to let the people of Bani Isra'il go. Prophet Musa ﷺ asked Allah to make his brother Harun ﷺ his helper. So, Allah granted Musa's wish and made his brother Harun ﷺ, who was also a Prophet, his helper and promised them both that they will win against Pharaoh.

Prophet Musa ﷺ and Prophet Harun ﷺ went to Pharaoh and told him to worship the One God, Allah. They told him he must let the Bani Isra'il go and to stop treating them badly, but Pharaoh did not want to listen. He did not believe that Prophet Musa ﷺ and Prophet Harun ﷺ were Allah's Prophets. He wanted them to show him a sign that they were really speaking the truth.

So, Prophet Musa ﷺ showed him the signs that Allah gave him, but Pharaoh still did not want to believe. He called Musa ﷺ a magician and told him that he will bring his own magicians to challenge him. They agreed on a date for this to happen and they gathered the people together to watch.

On the day of the challenge, Pharaoh's magicians got together and threw their sticks and ropes on the floor. The magicians tricked the people because it seemed that their sticks and ropes were moving like snakes. Prophet Musa ﷺ then threw his staff on the floor and it turned into a big snake, which ate all the small ones. When the Magicians saw this, they fell on the floor bowing before Prophet Musa ﷺ, because they knew this was a sign from the Lord of the Worlds, and it was not magic.

Seeing the Magicians accepting Allah as the Lord of the Worlds, Pharaoh got angry at them. He did not want to accept Prophet Musa ﷺ as a Prophet of Allah. He continued treating the Bani Isra'il badly. So, Allah sent more signs so that Pharaoh may believe and let the Bani Isra'il go.

Allah sent a plague to Pharaoh's people, and they could not benefit from the River Nile because its water had turned into blood. Allah sent them frogs and locusts and wherever the people went they could not get away from them. Every time Allah sent a sign, Pharaoh would promise to let the Bani Isra'il go, if Allah removed the punishment. But when the punishment was removed, Pharaoh broke his promise and he did not want to believe in Allah.

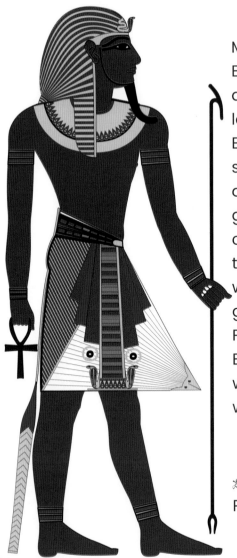

One day, Allah told Prophet Musa ﷺ to gather together the Bani Isra'il and to leave in the darkness of the night. They all left and made their way out of Egypt until they reached the sea shore. When Pharaoh found out about this, he got very angry and got his soldiers together and chased after the Bani Isra'il. When the Bani Isra'il saw that Pharaoh was coming with his army, they got worried, because they knew Pharaoh was going to kill them. But Prophet Musa ﷺ was not worried. He told them that Allah was with him.

Allah ordered Prophet Musa ﷺ to strike the sea with his staff. Prophet Musa ﷺ did as Allah had ordered him. When he struck the sea with his staff, the sea water parted in the middle and created a path which gave the Bani Isra'il way to cross the Red Sea.

The Bani Isra'il crossed the sea and reached to the other side safely. Pharaoh did not want the Bani Isra'il to escape so he chased them. While Pharaoh was running down the path, Allah ordered the sea to close the parting. The sea did as Allah commanded, and Pharaoh was drowned in the sea along with his army.

Allah showed the Bani Isra'il His power and might, and how He helps those who trust in Him and worship Him sincerely. To this day, the body of Pharaoh has been kept as a sign for all people till the Day of Judgement.

Sirah: The Business Trip to Syria

When Prophet Muhammad ﷺ was 25 years old, he was asked by Khadijah bint Khuwaylid to go to Syria on a business trip.

Khadijah bint Khuwaylid was a very good lady of the Quraysh tribe, and she was a rich business woman. The Quraysh were famous merchants; they would buy and sell things. They were

known for their famous trading trips twice a year, to Syria and Yemen.

Khadijah bint Khuwaylid wanted someone to go on this trip and sell her things for her. She heard of Prophet Muhammad ﷺ, because he was well known by everyone as 'al-Amin' (the trustworthy). She found out about the Prophet's good behaviour and manners, and she wanted the Prophet ﷺ to go on the trip and sell things for her.

The Prophet ﷺ travelled to Syria with her things that needed to be sold. He went with her young servant, called Maysarah.

When they reached a place called Bosra, in Syria, the Prophet ﷺ sat under a tree near a monastery.

A monk, who was living in the monastery, saw this and came rushing out. "Who is this man sitting under the tree?" he said to Maysarah.

"This man is from the Quraysh," Maysarah replied.

"No person sits under this tree except a prophet," the monk told Maysarah.

When they reached Syria, Prophet Muhammad ﷺ sold all of Khadijah's things. When they were returning to Makkah, it was very hot, and the sun was shining powerfully. Maysarah could see that the Prophet ﷺ was being protected from the sun by two angels and shaded by a cloud.

When he returned to Makkah, Maysarah told Khadijah everything that had happened. Hearing all of this she was very impressed, and she already knew about the excellent character of the Prophet ﷺ. So, because of this Khadijah bint Khuwaylid wanted to marry the Prophet ﷺ. Many men wanted to marry Khadijah, but she always said no to them.

The Prophet ﷺ and his uncle Hamzah went to Khadijah's father, Khuwaylid, and asked for them to get married. They got married, and they had six children together; two sons and four daughters.

The sons' names were Qasim and `Abdullah, but they died while they were young, before the announcement of Prophethood. The daughters' names were: Ruqayya, Zaynab, Umm Kulthum and Fatima – may Allah be pleased with them all.

The Prayer Positions - Part 1

The basic positions and the recitations are as follows.

1. Begin by facing the **Qiblah** (the direction of the Ka`bah) with your hands to your side.

2. **Niyyah**: Make an intention in your heart to offer the Salah for the sake of Allah.

3. **Takbir at-Tahrimah**: Raise your hands up to your ears, palms facing out, thumbs touching earlobes, and say the takbir:

Allaahu Akbar

اَللّٰهُ أَكْبَرُ

Allah is the greatest.

4. Qiyam: 'the Standing Position' – Fold your arms, right hand on top of the left hand.

During the Qiyam, we first recite the **Thana'** (Praise of Allah):

Subhaana-kallaa-humma wabi hamdika wa tabaara-kasmuka wa ta`aala jadduka wa laa ilaaha ghayruk

سُبْحَانَكَ اللّٰهُمَّ وَبِحَمْدِكَ وَتَبَارَكَ اسْمُكَ وَتَعَالَى جَدُّكَ وَلَا إِلٰهَ غَيْرُكَ

Glory be to You, O Allah, and all praises are due unto You. Blessed is Your name and high is Your majesty. None is worthy of worship but You.

Then we recite the **Ta`awwudh** (Seeking refuge in Allah):

A`oodhu billaahi minash-Shaytaanir-rajeem

أَعُوذُ بِاللهِ مِنَ الشَّيْطَانِ الرَّجِيْمِ

I seek Allah's protection from Satan, the rejected one.

Then we recite the **Tasmiyah** (In the Name of Allah):

Bismillaahir Rahmaanir Raheem

بِسْمِ اللهِ الرَّحْمٰنِ الرَّحِيْمِ

In the name of Allah, the Most Merciful, the Most Kind.

Then we recite **Surat al-Fatihah**:

Al-hamdu lillaahi Rabbil `aalameen. Ar-Rahmaanir Raheem. Maaliki yawmiddeen. Iyyaaka na`budu wa iyyaaka nasta`een. Ihdinas-siraatal mustaqeem. Siraatalladheena an`amta `alayhim; ghayril maghdubi `alayhim; waladdaal-leen.

اَلْحَمْدُ لِلّٰهِ رَبِّ الْعَالَمِيْنَ. اَلرَّحْمٰنِ الرَّحِيْمِ. مٰلِكِ يَوْمِ الدِّيْنِ. إِيَّاكَ نَعْبُدُ وَإِيَّاكَ نَسْتَعِيْنُ. اِهْدِنَا الصِّرَاطَ

الْمُسْتَقِيْمِ. صِرَاطَ الَّذِيْنَ أَنْعَمْتَ عَلَيْهِمْ غَيْرِ

الْمَغْضُوْبِ عَلَيْهِمْ وَلَا الضَّالِّيْنَ

All praise be to Allah alone, the Sustainer of all the worlds,
Most Compassionate, Ever-Merciful, Master of the Day
of Judgment. (O Allah!) You alone do we worship and to
You alone do we look for help. Show us the straight path;
the path of those upon whom You have bestowed Your
favours, not of those who have been afflicted with wrath,
nor of those who have gone astray.

Upon completing Surat al-Fatihah, we say '**Aameen**' quietly.
Then we recite a Surah from the Qur'an, such as **Surat al-Ikhlas**:

*Qul huwallaahu ahad; Allaahus-Samad. Lam yalid walam
yoolad. Walam yakullahu kufuwan ahad.*

قُلْ هُوَ اللّٰهُ أَحَدٌ. اَللّٰهُ الصَّمَدُ. لَمْ يَلِدْ وَلَمْ يُوْلَدْ. وَلَمْ

يَكُنْ لَّهُ كُفُوًا أَحَدٌ

(O Esteemed Messenger!) Proclaim: 'He is Allah, Who is
the One. Allah is the Self-Sufficient. He has no child, nor is
He born. Nor is there anyone equal to Him.'

5. **Ruku'**: 'the Bowing Position' – While saying the takbir, bow by bending forward until your back is flat like a table top. Place your hands on your knees and keep your arms straight. Then recite the following tasbih (glorification) three times:

Subhaana Rabbi-yal `Azeem

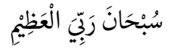

سُبْحَانَ رَبِّيَ الْعَظِيْمِ

Glory be to my Lord, the Great.

6. **Qawmah**: 'the Short Standing Position' – Stand up from the Ruku', with your hands by your sides. As you raise from the Ruku`, recite the following tasbih (glorification):

Sami'a Allaahu liman hamidah

سَمِعَ اللّٰهُ لِمَنْ حَمِدَهُ

Allah hears the ones who praise Him.

After raising from the Ruku`, recite the following tasbih (glorification) while in the standing position:

Rabbanaa lakal hamd

رَبَّنَا لَكَ الْحَمْدُ

Our Lord, all praise belongs to You.

The Prayer Positions - Part 2

7. Sajdah: 'First Prostration Position' – Saying the takbir, bow down further with both knees and hands on the ground with the head placed between the hands. The nose and forehead must touch the ground. Recite the following tasbih (glorification) three times:

Subhaana Rabbi-yal A`laa

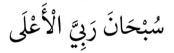

Glory be to my Lord, the Highest.

8. Jalsah: 'Short Sitting Position' – As you get up from the Sajdah, say the takbir. Sit for a short time on your knees, with your back straight and your hands on your thighs, facing down.

9. Sajdah: 'Second Prostration Position' – Same as 'First Prostration Position'.

10. **Qa'dah**: 'the Sitting Position' - Same as 'Short Sitting Position'. Recite the following:

During the Qa`dah we first recite the **Tashahhud** (Bearing Testimony):

At-Tahiyyaatu lillaahi was-salawaatu wattayyibaatu. As-salaamu `alayka ayyuhan-Nabiyyu warahmatullaahi wabarakaatuhu. As-salaamu 'alayna wa `alaa `ibaadillaahis saaliheen. Ash-hadu allaa ilaaha illallaahu wa ash-hadu anna Muhammadan `abduhu wa rasooluh.

اَلتَّحِيَّاتُ لِلهِ وَالصَّلَوَاتُ وَالطَّيِّبَاتُ.
اَلسَّلَامُ عَلَيْكَ أَيُّهَا النَّبِيُّ وَرَحْمَةُ اللهِ
وَبَرَكَاتُهُ. اَلسَّلَامُ عَلَيْنَا وَعَلَى عِبَادِ اللهِ
الصَّالِحِينَ. أَشْهَدُ أَنْ لَّا إِلهَ إِلَّا اللهُ
وَأَشْهَدُ أَنَّ مُحَمَّدًا عَبْدُهُ وَرَسُوْلُهُ

All prayers, salutations and goodness
are for Allah. Peace be upon you,
O Prophet, and Allah's mercy and
blessings be upon you. Peace be on us
and on all righteous servants of Allah.
I bear witness that no one is worthy of worship except
Allah and I bear witness that Muhammad is His (beloved)
servant and Messenger.

Note: While reciting the words '*Ash-hadu allaa ilaaha*' raise your index finger on your right hand, then put it down while reciting the words, '*illallaahu*'.

Then we recite the **Salat al-Ibrahimiyyah** (Abrahamic Salutation):

Allaahumma salli 'alaa Muhammadin wa `alaa Aali Muhammadin kamaa sallayta 'alaa Ibraaheema wa `alaa Aali Ibraaheema, innaka Hameedum Majeed. Allaahumma baarik 'alaa Muhammadin wa `alaa Aali Muhammadin kamaa baarakta 'alaa Ibraaheema wa `alaa Aali Ibraaheema, innaka Hameedum Majeed

اَللَّهُمَّ صَلِّ عَلَى مُحَمَّدٍ وَعَلَى آلِ مُحَمَّدٍ كَمَا صَلَّيْتَ عَلَى إِبْرَاهِيْمَ وَعَلَى آلِ إِبْرَاهِيْمَ، إِنَّكَ حَمِيْدٌ مَجِيْدٌ. اَللَّهُمَّ بَارِكْ عَلَى مُحَمَّدٍ وَعَلَى آلِ مُحَمَّدٍ كَمَا بَارَكْتَ عَلَى إِبْرَاهِيْمَ وَعَلَى آلِ إِبْرَاهِيْمَ، إِنَّكَ حَمِيْدٌ مَجِيْدٌ

O Allah! Send peace on (the Holy Prophet) Muhammad and on the family of (the Holy Prophet) Muhammad just as you sent peace on Ibrahim and on the family of Ibrahim. Surely, you are Most Praiseworthy, the Exalted. O Allah! Send your blessings on (the Holy Prophet) Muhammad and the family of (the Holy Prophet) Muhammad, just as you sent blessings on Ibrahim and the family of Ibrahim. Surely, you are Most Praiseworthy, the Exalted.

Then recite the following **Du`a**:

Rabbij 'alni muqeemas salati wa min dhurriyati Rabbanaa wa taqabbal du`aa. Rabbanaghfir li wa li-waalidayya wa lil-mu'mineena yawma yaqumul hisaab.

رَبِّ اجْعَلْنِي مُقِيمَ الصَّلَاةِ وَمِنْ ذُرِّيَّتِيْ

رَبَّنَا وَتَقَبَّلْ دُعَاءِ. رَبَّنَا اغْفِرْ لِي وَلِوَالِدَيَّ وَلِلْمُؤْمِنِيْنَ

يَوْمَ يَقُوْمُ الْحِسَابُ

O Lord! Make me and my children steadfast in the Salah. Our Lord! Accept my prayer. Our Lord! Forgive me and my parents and the believers on the Day of Judgement.

11. **Salam**: 'The Ending Position' – End the prayer by turning your head towards the right shoulder and then the left shoulder and saying the following greeting in each direction.

As-Salaamu `alaykum wa rahmatullaah.

اَلسَّلَامُ عَلَيْكُمْ وَرَحْمَةُ اللّٰهِ

Peace be upon you (all) – and the mercy of Allah.

Du'a Before Sleeping

اَللّٰهُمَّ بِاسْمِكَ أَمُوتُ وَأَحْيَا

O Allah, in Your Name, I die and come to life.

Du'a When Waking Up

اَلْحَمْدُ لِلّٰهِ الَّذِيْ أَحْيَانَا بَعْدَ مَا أَمَاتَنَا وَإِلَيْهِ النُّشُوْرُ

All praise be to Allah, Who gave us life after causing us to die, and to Him is the raising (after we die).

The Sunnah manners BEFORE sleeping:

1. Brush your teeth.

2. Perform Wudu'.

3. Make sure you have read all the five prayers for the day.

4. Clean your bed.

5. Think about your day, thanking Allah for all the good things, and asking for His forgiveness for any mistakes you might have made.

6. Read the Du'a before sleeping.

The Sunnah manners DURING sleep:

1. Sleep on the right side of your body.

2. Place your right hand under your face, resting your right cheek on the right palm.

3. Do not sleep on your stomach.

The Sunnah manners of AWAKENING from sleep

1. Read the Du'a when you wake up.

2. Thank Allah for giving you another day to worship Him and ask Him to help you throughout the day.

3. Make a good intention for the day.

Belief in Allah's Books

In the beginning, all the people — the children of Prophet Adam ﷺ — were part of one nation. Everyone believed in Allah and worshipped Him alone. Shaytan did not like this. He wanted to misguide people and keep them away from worshipping Allah.

Some people listened to Shaytan. These people wanted money and power, and they did not want to be kind to other people. They forgot the message that was given to them by their great-grandfather Prophet Adam ﷺ. They forgot about Paradise and Hell, and the life hereafter.

These people lost the knowledge that Prophet Adam ﷺ had given them. The Shaytan whispered in the hearts of these people telling them to change Prophet Adam's message, and in this way, he misguided them. He told them to make idols and worship them.

Some people listened to the Shaytan, but the people who stuck to the truth understood that worshipping idols was wrong. They were guided by Allah and they told the other people not to worship false gods, but they did not listen.

The people split into two groups. One group was the people who believed in Allah and worshipped Him alone, and the other group was the people who disobeyed Allah and worshipped idols.

Allah did not want the people to be misguided. So, He sent His Prophets and Messengers to them. The Prophets and Messengers were Allah's special servants and they told people what was right and wrong. They told the people not to follow Shaytan and not to worship idols.

Allah gave the Prophets and Messengers special messages. These special messages are known as '**revelation**'. In these 'revelations', Allah gave knowledge to the Prophets and Messengers, who then passed that knowledge on to their people.

Those who believed and followed the Prophets became the believers, while those who did not believe in them became the disbelievers. Allah rewarded the believers and He punished the disbelievers.

Allah wanted to keep on guiding the people to the truth after the Prophets and Messengers passed away. So, He revealed holy books to them as a source of guidance for their people.

These holy books contained all kinds of knowledge and explained to the people how to live a good and righteous life. The people received guidance from these holy books and used them to know what was right and wrong. These holy books gave rules for the people to follow in their lives.

There were **four** important books revealed by Allah to the Prophets. They were:

01 At-Tawrah (The Torah)

This book was revealed to Prophet Musa ﷺ. It was a book of law for the Bani Isra'il.

02 Az-Zabur (The Psalms)

This book was revealed to Prophet Dawud ﷺ. It contained many poems, prayers and religious songs.

03   Al-Injil (The Gospel)

This book was revealed to Prophet 'Isa ﷺ. It was a book of law and stories that taught many lessons. It had many of the teachings of the Tawrah and confirmed them to be true.

04   Al-Qur'an

This is the last and final book, which was revealed to Prophet Muhammad ﷺ. It confirmed the central message of all the past books.

Apart from the four holy books, Allah sent many smaller books called '**scrolls**' (**suhuf**). These included the scrolls sent to Prophet Ibrahim ﷺ.

NOTES

NOTES